CROWED

Splash of coffee
like a Rorschach
head of a crow—
Upended, turned
sideways, beak
extended toward
the sun, dripping
honey and mayhem.

—Michael Magee

CROWED
Michael Magee

MoonPath Press

Poetry
ISBN 978-1-970256-03-1

Cover art: *Celtic Knot* by Sadie Murazzo

Title page art: *Crowed*, paper collage by Sadie Murazzo

Back cover author photo by Peter Curiel
with assistance from NewProfile.com

Book design by Tonya Namura using Minion Pro

MoonPath Press, an imprint of Concrete Wolf Poetry Series,
is dedicated to publishing the finest poets
living in the U.S. Pacific Northwest.

MoonPath Press
c/o Concrete Wolf
PO Box 2220
Newport, OR 97365-0163

MoonPathPress@gmail.com

https://MoonPathPress.com

in the words of poets, friends, and family,
the lives that inspired me to write these poems

TABLE OF CONTENTS

I. CROWED

CROWED

I
CROWED

My heart is like a singing bird.
—Hanif Kureishi, quoting Christina Rossetti's
"A Birthday"

IRELAND'S EYE

I am the eye of Ireland
 from where I watch
the east is always at my back,
Howth raises its head of heather
to flower into thistle and gorse.

I sight beyond Martello towers
to the north, white sands flowing
 into wheat, fields that rise
to Tara's Hill where the throne sits
 empty for a thousand years.

To the south I see the sun,
 most holy emblem, encircling
masts of ships to form St. Patrick's Cross,
 may their own good fisher sons
sailing on this tide never be lost.

 To the west I follow storms
banished beyond the Shannon
 to see them settle on Ben Bulben
 or rain like stones on Knocknarea
where Maeve's proud bull runs free.

ROAD TO GALWAY

Five miles from the city it begins to rain,
I walk the soft margin of the road
with my stick to lean on for a walking cane
past caravans and trails of gypsy camps,
the laundry hung out in waves to dry.
I've come from Coole Park and Thoor Ballylee
and am haunted not so much by Yeats
as blind Raftery and dead Mary Hynes.

So the rain is no sorrow to me today,
but I bear the weather as a brother,
the sight of the bay is enough for now.
A few children playing by the road stare
at my army raincoat, tweed cap and wildflowers
like a man who has found his way home
from the pub after too many hours.

And I enter old Galway near Claddagh Quay
towards the dock and the bay where a woman
at Stella's Café directs me to No. 19.
There an Irish Spencer Tracy lets me in
brings my wet things for the line
and I feel my breath coming back to me
like swans on the tide.

THIRTEEN SWANS

I

Thirteen swans on the tide in Galway Harbor
   float along the quay in single file,
     the water runs against them,
the swans drift, a salmon jumps ahead
  toward the Spanish Arches, a flotilla
near where Fitzstephen, mayor in 1493
executed his son for killing a Spaniard
all for a maiden's handkerchief of tears.
  The swans mingle, fluffing their tails,
bobbing for fish, dipping while the tide's out,
   taking communion in the shallow water
where fishermen and poets drop their lines
beneath the Salmon Weir along the Claddagh.

II

A swan arches itself, half out of water
     in a mermaid's pose
  on the canal beneath Salt Hill.
I walk through the Spanish Arches
  home to the old side of Galway
where Irish-speaking seamen lived
and breathed in their heady Gaelic.
I stay near Claddagh Quay with Monaghan,
  his wife and son, a family known to all.

III

Tonight he offers us a nightcap,
poteen from potato skins that Peegan Mike
served up for moonshines in the *Playboy*.
And waterlogged with a heavy head
I float like a barrel into bed.

SOFT VERGES

We have come to observe
this divination of sky
hoping we will merge
along the road's soft verges
with snow-in-summer beside us
and try to gather ourselves
like the sheep who fade away.
Swallows dart into our headlights,
at each turn we are surprised,
no one asks us why we've come
to where this fold runs away,
the tip overgrown with foliage
where even these cows stand holy.

In the blue of subtle evening
fish jump at our shadows,
we cast across the stream,
a lamb parted from its mother's side
looks lost and wonders at us
with our bouquets of cow parsley
we have gathered for May weddings.
We are drifting home through
narrow lanes, always giving way
to what's ahead, a wave
to the evening's still blessing
here on the cusp of June.

Pastures, fields, four-square gardens,
rows of lettuce, cabbage heads,
spring onion, the flowers' stalks
of golden rape, bright poppies,
boasts of pigs on grunting farms,
barracks of their Quonset huts,
the ditches of moat and bailey,

hills of incontrovertible dirt
against breezing waterfalls of grass
the wind blows through like shot silk.
All of this, rising and falling
to the tide of a red sunset.

OFF THE HOOK

They're tying the fishing line with nylon,
spreading out their tackle in the living room,
with packages of mealworms, and fish eggs,
they have the creel, the dog who fetches your socks
who sits by the river never moving a muscle,
with their rain gear, wellies, ponchos and tents,
they've been ready for hours, risen silent
before first light like King Richard, assembling
and reassembling troops of fishing nets, plotting
out their encampment, #167 near Gunthorpe Bridge
with maps and compasses, a torch for light,
they're tapping and whistling, having a laugh.

Now the dogs are barking, they've packed bags
under their eyes, found the moon down the road
past the soft verges, over the potholes
where they'll wait for barbel and bass, hoping
for the big ones, instead getting carp,
throwing the small fry back, with the nose of Sally
the German Shorthair. If they don't strike
it's the fault of those bloody fish,
who are always going bloody elsewhere for bait,
and they'll instead tell stories of old men
by the river who knew their beds well enough:
the man from Poland who was a spy, he could tell
you well enough where to drop a line, where after the rain
they'd come open-mouthed to the surface, so ready
to be taken, you won't even need to fight.

ARRESTED GOLDFINCH

I hold you in my hands
your sleek yellow breast.
Here, you are silenced
into shock from the window—
a glass half empty.

As I pick you up, cupped
in my palms, I wondered
what stillness brings
in your green shadow
your little body, cold.

What could I add or
subtract from you, mouth
agape, eyes bright dots.
Most of all, could there
be life, if I kept you warm
cradled in a woolen hat.

Could I massage your heart
rubbing your feathers sleek
to bring you back, perhaps
our lives were meant to meet
just in this way, between
sky and earth, mid-flight.

As you lay behind the toaster
to keep warm before
I let you go to see if given
a pulse you could flutter
away, I only know
my lips are sealed for now.

FROM A SCREEN SAVER

On a peninsula that expresses itself
where cattle wear holy faces
Highland cattle hold up the sky
with their horned antlers
tilting the edge, a rocking cradle
where shepherds nearby
tend earth and sky, grazing
like the cattle, wide-eyed
we give ourselves a sheep's permission
to accompany their nodding heads
where the waves are shields
and the cattle's bells keep ringing
in the drover's head.

OLDE ENGLISH TEACHER

A bit hidebound, dog-eared
who writes a letter
a bit harebrained too
his parchment skin
turned over into crisp
white linen—but
no ruffled collar—
3 o' clock scholar
who composes sonnets
to his dead white lover
there is an end to every
sad song, a newly born writer.
There is a bird that sings
on every limb, a song to give.

FLICKER

I rose to a robin's song
a flicker in light-pink frock appeared
winked speckles flew limb to limb
sounding its warning echoes
which warned me not to move.

I adjusted my sight to see
a cross in midair waxing like a cedar
and waning as I knew its call—
a sonar reading height and depth
on my radar screen.

Cries instead of little pings as it flew
high toward the crown, a glimpse
before it's gone just to remind
us on the ground
of what beauty lives up there.

CROWED

Today I saw a dead crow
shiny on the sidewalk
lying on its curved back
like a raincoat, a city slicker
that had come to rest
its wings splayed apart.

Like an emblem in the dark
surrounded by gray as if the bird
in it had flown away
and left us here with this vest—
a soft imitation of what
had passed, its dark nest.

Tossed away while I wondered
where was the bird wearing it?
Sharp-eyed needlework
and full of fight and flight without
its black oil-slickered jacket
left behind zipper broken.

Was it laughing at us somewhere
on the edge of creation, cackling
at death, a joke at our expense.
Somewhere beyond our thinking—
is a blackness where the crow
has swallowed even the sunlight.

BEHOLD THE MAN

Ecce Homo *(1605–1609)*
From an article by Ingrid D. Rowland

In Caravaggio's painting, we see Christ
almost in spirit form escaping
life bled out of him as he clutches
his scepter, eyes closed, dreaming
beyond while dark-bearded Pilate
seems but an instrument of the state.

Palms open as if pleading mercy.
Murder is in the air, blood rampant
an act of judgment to be made
as Christ keeps mum, his corporeal
body shining, the only thing left
to behold.

NUMEROLOGY

Everyone who came
was a friend or a flower,
those with mates, singles
and children, matched pairs.

Beanies, bald heads,
flat hats, women with chokers,
well-coiffed hair, earrings,
smiling loafers in plaids.

Each had a chair
to sit in, unpaid—
the room grew quiet
until the pop of the mic.

The poet began to read,
the room listened, and one by one
they came to stand, observe
and be counted.

GRANDMAS

They look alike in oval frames
some Norwegian, some German
like Hazel, rounded-square, severe-
looking silver-gelatin hair
pulled tight around their faces
so they'll fit into the frames.
Hardworking, full of families
cataracts in their eyes, they see
through the past—all of them dutiful
and bound to their thin husbands
bound to clear from their sight
to a pool hall, the tavern
off-shift after they wander home
back to their sepia-tone lives.

BALLAD OF MY GRANDFATHER'S LINOTYPE

There he is cast-iron character,
my grandfather and progenitor
rakish cigarette tucked in his mouth.

Slicked-back patent leather hair
squint-eyed Bulldog Drummond
of the linotype machine decked out

in braces, strapped to a wooden chair
a tin of Prince Albert "roll-your-own"
at his elbow, the sage of Wapato.

Silver-tongued prophet of the sports page
looking up from the linotype tray
through twinkling rimless glasses.

Cow back home in the barn, pail and stool
my grandmother brought to the pool hall
to milk where he was shooting billiards.

In the background, bones of a radiator
shiny as though they'd been picked clean
by the vultures of self-esteem.

Ready for business with his gooseneck lamp
caught in this photo in mid-sentence
before this final inky paragraph.

MY MOTHER'S SINGER MACHINE

Black and golden filigree script
"Singer" with a foot treadle
rocking back and forth my sins of wear
sing like a cradle song to me
small walnut drawers in swirls
with little knobs and bobbins
threaded spools jiggling time.

Playing out their lives that twirl
around her little finger still
pulling tight while the needle
works up and down, cross-stitching
strokes that shake the wooden
framework of her hobbyhorse.

A zither's tight strings plucked and pulled,
everything planted in her sewing basket
will be on earth as in heaven held fast
with golden threads, her signature
in silver needles, the sound of
buttons sewn in place unto death.

GHOST

My mother's paper-thin face
in a black-pencil line drawing,
smoky as charcoal to the touch,
keeps haunting me.

Just as my fingers follow among
the contours and trace the scent
of her body's perfume, dry, warm
as her parchment skin.

I want to hold her up like a cameo,
her half-moon smile appears,
so my thoughts feel her pulse
rise from its spirit place.

A neap tide pulls at my feet,
that carries her away from me
as I see her floating somewhere
in the mothlike darkness.

AT THE DOG HOUSE

(The rib eye steak
tenderness not guaranteed)

Tenderness was never guaranteed,
the rib eye steak that bit you back,
even for those with no teeth
who put their canes on the bar,
who could drink double vodka martinis,
sing along with Dick Dickerson's organ
playing "In the Good Old Summertime."

The little old ladies with blue hair,
lantern-jawed cabbies, spent bookies,
schoolteachers, lawyers, no-accountants,
reporters still learning to bend elbows,
while waitresses with beehive hairdos
and don'ts stood over you clicking teeth,
each one carrying her own Tabasco sauce.

It was always midnight in the back
room, kewpie dolls stuffed in behind
the cash register, pinball machines,
their rocker arms flipping out losers.
No one could make head or tail of
the dog wagging its ticktock, the check
came unannounced like a slap on the back.

It was a place you'd take your mother
but not your girlfriend, or show up
alone, sitting at the counter, drinking
your coffee black. It never mattered
when and if the sun came out, "Honey,"
if you walked in that door the waitresses
were always guaranteed to talk back.

AT THE WOMEN'S UNIVERSITY CLUB

Mixed in with grace, the wassail punch bowl is overflowing,
brings pink color to our cheeks while women in red
with reindeer antlers on their heads and Santa stocking caps
move among us with angel hair and bright greeting-card faces.

In the basement, the opera singers raise toasts from *Tosca*,
sing Neapolitan courting songs taught to them by their fathers
as we chosen few men sit next to our ladies, outnumbered
100-1 with courtly stares under the gazes of matronly
    paintings.

The room is festooned, so full of decoration and cheer, the
    women,
like little winter wrens, practice their songs in two-part
    inventions,
looking on as we imperfect males: fathers, lovers, sons, all
    attend,
trying to do justice in the name of our diminished species.

AFTER

I have been made a long time ago
from splinters of my being
and polished bone bearing my weight
as though I was a cedar chest
filled with remains, told me where
I might lie among old sofas, underwear.

Antimacassars crocheted for me
by my grandmother rest her soul,
my grandfather's lineage, caught
in my wild oats I eat each day
yet here I am still breathing fine
linen, encased in the pale skin
or is it foreskin of my ancestors.

AT PEACE ON THE KLICKITAT

The photo of the model was taken in April;
she was murdered in October.

Yes, she seemed to fit
  angled on the steep slope
a nude lying on her side.

Under that grove of trees
  but hanging on only by
the long roots of her hair.

Here may she rest
  so young and unaware
uncovered by the fact

Of her death while she
  still ripens at the loss
vulnerable as fruit.

Her body in repose
  not yet starting the slide
that gravity takes.

Far from the trees
  delivered inconveniently
from death.

FALLEN

The torso of the birch tree
like a toppled statue
remains to be seen—less
the sum of its parts.

Now, its enormous arms like
a blacksmith, legs and ankles
stumps as anvils, no head
as though executed by a king
some remnant of the living.

Decapitated, arms torn away
revealing the red insides,
its sawdust heart, illuminated
in December light, over which
as I stumble among the bones
no man cried for.

DEAD END

Dead rise from the ashes of the California wildfires
the man with a hose found in Altadena.

What flame retardant could have saved him from
blowback on a street whose name became obliterated?

Where there are no addresses, no street signs
to tell who lived here, a doorbell still rings

and a basketball hoop without a backboard
where every street is a dead end.

Now it's all retreat and boxed in not boxwood valleys
where cars are abandoned, melted down to the axles.

No Will Rogers Ranch, or Topanga Ranch Motel, or even
playgrounds, churches, only whistles of sirens of wind

blow through the ghost town of the Pacific Palisades,
and driftwood of what remains in Malibu.

POSTCARD FROM OSAKA

for Al

The cherry trees leave me
weak-kneed, Osaka Castle
with its many sloping roofs above
the stonewall, its flecked pattern
looks soft as brocade.

While the letters "Osaka" rise
on walking stilts, and I am
moved to see the yellow thrush
singing on its perch, a stamp
imprinted in the corner.

"Air Mail" in paler blue fades
like a vapor trail to disappear.
Below the dragon island awaits,
while my card on the windowsill
hangs like a Chinese lantern.

THE VIOLINIST

A violinist,
   he cradles violin and bow
      hand on chin, studies the score.

Hair shiny, neatly combed and
   parted, his country divided
      scarred with bombs and war.

Yet, he's composed. How music
   focuses the soul, tunes you in
      to see what you can control.

What's in play, his fingers obey
   the way he functions, pauses
      ready for the next attack.

WOODEN CROSS

I look at the wooden grooves
    like arrows pointing
      to a rabbit's fur

Wooden altar of a tabletop
    wonder if my touch
    would redeem it

Its grain keeps me even
    may have landed at
  my elbows perpendicular

To this wooden cross
    that grounds me with
    a stain of varnish.

OLD GROWTH

"Old growth can be a reminder of a resource too."
—*Seattle Times*

Too tough to cut, original
as the forest we are alone in
an old-growth forest grows
as our timbered words echo
we find our light years' rings
roots have anchored themselves
created canopies, flickers of
a life we knew before
chain saws took out our forest
overcame our lumbered brethren
came, a second generation
stronger than before and somehow
I survived surrounded by those
who kept me young inside
as I grew older, instead became
its old master.

OYSTERVILLE

Here in the red grass, I look for mountains
of oysters too numerous to count, ridges of
white sharp as razor blades, for seagulls to
cover the sky, like vultures, where surveyors
have plaited the land, a lone tractor sits in its
traces, and the sign announces there are to be
condominiums down the road near the Espey
House named for the founder of the town
whose son grew up here, gathering all
the words he could muster to fill a book, collector
of more than mussels, *gapers* and *littlenecks*.

Here, there must be stories to tell, for
in the church there are flyers (one per family)
promising every Saturday the Shoalwater
Storytellers will come passing on their skeins
of history. Next Thursday the school is having
a chili feed, but who can wait, not the car full
of tourists asking the way to the restaurant
that doesn't exist. Their mother needs a
bathroom, "Quick!" We must leave Oysterville
too, no richer than we came, only surmising
the lore, silent as the grasses, and the church
bell that never rings. We leave as we came,
empty-handed, ready to be shucked again.

ALONG THE WATERFRONT

With the poets and birds installed
more artwork is on the way
posts and beams stacked up
an installation of the wind
sculptures of salmon that
follow the river, canoe work
above the Salish Sea from
La Push to Golden Gardens
goes on the chain of knowledge.

There will be cane baskets
sculptures yet to come
longhouses, revealed,
dream catchers nets for poems.
Woven beads and blankets
with ravens' beaks pointing
toward true north, salmon
bursting the banks through
turnstiles of logs, basket weavers
salmon song, posts and beams
along which you may go
without a paddle to get home.

BREAKING CAMP

She takes a branch beating back
the refuse, squalor of shopping bags
and leaves like lovers trying to tie them
to her shopping cart with bungee cords
and strings attached, he sweeping
the stairs hard work as they collect
their rubbish charred bits of wood
armed with tarp, parts of their bivouac
he battles with a branch like Don Quixote.

To her Sancho Panza, a windmill of arms
turning heads, sending up smoke signals
in sooty clouds above them like bad angels
breaking camp in a ring of hell, Beelzebub
had just left, trying to recollect
their lost lost souls, they neaten the sidewalk
a legacy smoothed like a grader,
as he combs through the bushes like he
is reaping a field of wheat, she a model housewife.

BENCH WARRANT

A woman in pink and black
removes herself from a bench
like an Amazon Prime bag
sleeping on its side before
a gust of wind picks it up
and runs across the street
and she is rising on her own
after last night's collapse
the wind gone out of her
turned over like a blanket
in a doorway tucked inside
waiting to get out, a girl
curled half in shadow
like a leaf.

CROSSING TO NOWHERE

In Kansas, a crossing to nowhere
a jurisdiction of dust and scarecrows
in cornfields in the open air
where nothing in the world moves
the hunters' words keep to themselves
in the muted mouths of crows
dust and disorder far as the eye can stare,
a target of bullseyes made from silos
threshers and wind farms,
the sprinklers *kachew, kachew,*
a mist made of sparrows
and sunflowers and overalls
that don't bust no matter
who wears them in or out in any kind
of weather, vain hope of rain
where the highways turn blue.

II
IN HISTORICAL ACCENTS

The first thing I loved was that it (the book) smelled of
Freshly printed paper.
—Rember Yahuarcani, *Buinaima's Dream*

SEA DEEP IN BLUE INK

Tonight, the white ministerial
moon keeps track—
all on accounting blue-lined paper-thin
on the surface
under the goose-necked lamp
that precious ink that flows—
for it never sleeps on the
other side of its pillow—
watching instead from the top
of my window, opalescent cool
as a cat's collegial eye, staring in
so I do not stray under
its observation.

Writing word for word some poem
of little note to anyone but me
for in its Confucian wisdom
it lets me be, not interfering
thinking I am amused in this cell
of my room, totally blinkered in
seeing only the wide dead sea
ahead of me, wave after wave
of blue line approaching—
as I try to see above it all, but sink
back and let its crest catch hold as
my iris floats on its little life raft
hoping for rescue to come along
in the shape of a period.

SONG SPARROW

Its round body swelling
as it sings, fills the air
with clear notes as I
try to speak in my own.

Slow down, so I can hear
the bushtits full of sound
a little choir of voices
comes from a thicket

of one ready to be found
among the nondescript
overgrowth where
all you hear is song.

FREDERIC, LORD LEIGHTON'S ELEGY

Now that you've turned your head,
birds can be quiet, a still point,
your sadness in brown and white,
light and shadow, no respite.
A calm comes over you, what
can you be grieving for,
a past that is history, a present
going nowhere. In the future
you will look back on this and wonder
what it was you remembered.
By then it will already be too late.

HEIGHTS OF ABRAHAM

From here a camera couldn't register
the drop from Abraham's heights.
You can't believe a world exists
beyond the peaks and dales of Derbyshire.
You graze like a sheep on the hills,
resting your eye, if you had a hymnal
you would sing like a Welsh choir.

No shepherd to shout you down,
just wind that swirls around you
on this keep, holding up the dome
of sky, sweeping the horizon line
come storms, the kings of the mountains
must live here who hold their breath
then blow you out.

MARSH ANGELICA

for Jean

"This is the latest of our umbelliferous plants
to come into bloom."

I see you in the garden
pulling up loose weeds on hands and near
your bucket and clippers near,
or pruning among the rose bushes,
clearly, the whiteness in your hair.
You are wondering where I am
when I will appear among the poppies
gone to seed, or with the mower
offer to lend a helping hand.

This has always been our season
when we took country rides,
gathered heat from the leaves,
felt the snap of Autumn coldness.
I think you are wrapping the faucets
your jacket pink as fuchsias.
As always you're nearest the sun,
our fruits have yet to ripen.

Rushing through the mountain ash
I hear the wind blessing us,
see the masts of branches bobbing
wondering why you aren't beside me
as I pick blackberries, pulling
away the tops of spent hydrangeas.
I have come across an ocean to live
in England. I open your letters
and gather the clippings.

BIRDCAGE WALK

Resting here among elderberry
and bay willow herb
the lords and ladies
have already gone to seed.
Listen, the rose hips
have already opened,
and wind rushes through
the wild blackberries
that keep you in thrall.

You spend your time
taking samples in old crisps bags
to puzzle over, and after
you have finished untangling hair,
analyzing the moles on your skin,
counting insect bites,
and digging for dirt
beneath your fingernails, you wonder.

Are these spots before your eyes
or deadly nightshade?
Is that metal rusting in
the field inside your blood?
Is there peace among morning glories
fighting for the sun?
Or is salvation found
in the moaning of a rock dove?

CROMWELL'S PROCESSIONAL

Of butchers, coupage, corpses
of meat and mutton, pink pig
the heart of the sheep and he
a blacksmith's boy who beats
design out of metal to make
it shine, brat of Lambeth
to be made Knight of the Garter
ascend to his rightful place from
Walter of Putney all along the Thames
he raises his head and where
they lower the bridge instead
and bows his bullish
but not papal neck, arise
Thomas to your calling, you
have been handmade by Henry,
Lord of Maidenhead, but not Regent
yet, that depends on Queen Jane.

QUEEN JANE'S DEATH

I weep for the death of Queen Jane.
Henry didn't, the forecast cruel
and Cromwell thinks, "I could have done
better than this," yet she fades
white as a milkmaid no succor
for her birth pains, but delivery
what's left, the little prince
survives, while his mother waits
like a new moon about to rise again
in a grave. No regrets for queens, soon
they'll be another sad end for Jane's
suffering is over, life will be restored,
as though she barely existed,
"a lily among the roses" as Henry said.

REVISITING BYRON; NEWSTEAD ABBEY

Rusting sword fern,
the green islands of chlorophyll
in dead oak leaves,
cars pass on the road with their
headlights in processional.

Two women walk like pilgrims,
with a dog on the lead,
we pass the cricket ground where men
chase a ball among the leaves.

There are satyrs in the garden,
Dionysus or Pan holding grapes
but someone has "gotten the goat"
of the female deity.

We sit "totting up" in the courtyard,
watching the peacocks parade
their long tails, and listen
to the sweetness of chaffinches.

Later we read the praise of Byron
for his dog, whom he loved
more than any man, and was more
faithful to than any woman.

SHAKE HANDS WITH THE CRUSADER

"If you shake the Crusader's hand, it brings you luck."
—Patrick McGrath

In the vault of St. Michan's Church
I shook the Crusader's hand,
feeling his palm like polished oak.
The curator told of a spiderweb
hanging like silk, for a hundred years
in the doorway to the tomb, until
an American tourist touched it,
then it crumbled like a moth into dust.
Nearby are twin coffins side by side,
brothers Sheares who were drawn and quartered
by the British during the 1798 Rebellion.

But a man who stood seven feet tall
could not be put to rest so easily,
his legs had to be broken, forced
into his pelvis to fit the coffin.
His skeleton's broad shoulders betray
his stature, the fingers long as talons.
He is buried with a nun half his size,
all year their remains are preserved
in fifty-two-degree temperatures, sealed
in a dry cell; before we left and darkness
eclipsed us, I wished him luck.

THE ILLUSION OF HARRY KELLAR'S
HEAD GIVEN TO HARRY HOUDINI ON
ANTIQUES ROADSHOW

A piece of hardwood floats above the table
with otherworldly eyes
pupils missing, hollowed out like
an empty magician's hat
his vision a gift to his friend
a conjuring trick left behind for him
remains after the shipwreck
when he lost all his props,
those mesmerizing eyes that stare
out from the sphere of his head.

He elevates himself from a pedestal
to hover over Houdini, a reminder
of what cannot be reduced to gimmickry
or indirection, even in this a temporal
world of illusion—instead—
a floating incarnation of the cerebral
power of a magician suspended like
a laser image of Harry Kellar, the
great man with wonder looks on through
the powerful wave of the living hand.

CITY OF WHISPERS

A man singing to his milk bottle
on the stoop, lets his voice ring
chatting up the world or arguing
with a cow he's never seen.

Another twitching in his chair
in a café, crossing and uncrossing
his legs, makes up his patter
that spills from the newspaper.

The sane among us barely speak,
sit knees-up on buses,
trying to avoid each other's eyes.
We keep our words inside.

But somehow they escape
past corners of our mouths.
Rumors are only the lies
we tell ourselves.

THE POET'S CLOTHES

Why should he dress any better
when his hands are tied by lines,
who breaks bread together
shuffles this pack of lies.

Still he is fine enough
to merit a peacock feather
yet all his fine embroideries
won't change even the weather.

PAUL DUNBAR, "ELEVATOR BOY"

I know why the caged poet
sings, of "Oak and Ivy" with
his golden braids and buttons.

Who has wings, then folds them
against the bars, spreads wide
across the page to get passengers

coming and going up and down.
Paul plies his trade, waiting
for a moment, writer in vernacular

of the south, the songs of Negroes
meanwhile at the Callahan Power Building
home of National Cash Register.

He is in sympathy with those
who are clipped and forced to sing
slave melodies: "*When Malindy sings*"

he writes for those who kick out
their legs, adjust their strut
from the Tenderloin to New Orleans.

"Jump back, Honey, jump back"
as his words take flight to dance
across the floor—a "Cakewalk"

DYLAN THOMAS AT THE GATE

His head turned in three-quarter profile,
back arched, in this photograph the writer
is caught in the act of poetic martyrdom
pressed against the bars of his escape.

If he had somewhere to go, he would—
a man less clever would surrender by now
in these sepia tones surrounding him,
the leaves crashing down at his feet.

Poised as though awaiting a life sentence
there is no other sound to be heard,
only a man on the listening ground
guarding his cage of words.

LEAVING NEWARK

Hay is braided in the fields,
long shadows, the train
slowing at Newark Castle,
too early for the exotic dancer,
a dark-eyed flash in a photograph,
the windows of the depot are boarded,
the test results are in,
and England have lost again.

The crops already harvested,
a time for leavings,
where the sun moves through
in lace leaves, the sky
pale as laundry soap.
The only hope for me
are fields turned and plaited
fresh as a duvet.

Cabbage, broccoli, cauliflower
all come to advantage,
in a twist of the river,
the last swatch of the sun
in winking headlights,
a horse grazing in its shadow.
Six red fire buckets wait
at Lowdham Station, but no
brigade meets us as we pass.
Starlings scatter overhead,
in a flurry of ashes,
the wind sends no regrets.

THE SUBTLE KNOT

for Ben Drake
(in memoriam, 1933–2025)

"As our blood labours to beget
  Spirits, as like soules as it can,
Because such fingers need to knit
  That subtle knot, which makes us man."
        —John Donne

I

"I would have lived and died for you."
How could any lover keep those vows,
for every one of us settles for less:
love's not a matter of life and death.
There is not breath enough, the heart
stops short; our hands can only caress
digging deep within our empty pockets.
And moments in bed make dead awakenings
confronted with the daily keeping house,
the closing hand that won't reveal itself;
and our untended minds need weeding out.
What we settle for is hardest to take,
our lovers made the objects of our hate,
and disappointments that we all must suffer,
the falling into debt, the faithless lover.
These subtle measurements of gain and loss
weigh against the urging of each promise.

II

Lovers shed no light, love has no answers,
what can lovers assemble by their prayers,
face to face between the closing sheets,

arms clinging to arms, bodies going under,
cries and countercries of warmth and pain,
the dark and sudden running of our blood;
then the dying, falling resolution.
The sun withdraws and we must fill a room,
and parting from the darkness of each other
we face the mirror an unconcealed life,
common as work and sitting down to supper
or laying on of hands to rub the shoulders;
we hurt and heal, our words invoke no priest.
What draws us here is so much deeper
than testaments of living and dying after.
These then constitute the only secrets;
just cleaning house, getting love to work.

III

"I would have lived and died for you."
Let go of that dated, worn-out crucible,
it is not the test of loving we know.
On this firm trust we make our claim,
that love's our benefactor only in name.
We will love within this simple proposal
sharing of the all too humanly possible.

COME LIVE WITH ME AND BE MY LOVE:
A SIMPLE SWAIN IN A TIME OF CORONAVIRUS

Excuse me for coming to your door
but I'm looking for a maid of any age
to traipse about with and gather flowers
for the disaffected and extremely bored.

We'll jump the cracks on the sidewalk,
it's just a lark for now and could become
full-time employment if I find enough
work to make ends meet, so to speak.

A minute of your time to chat you up
or anyone else around the house who
isn't busy, I'm trying to make my way through
life; it's not a ploy but honest work.

Until I get a government check
to keep me occupied and out of mischief,
idle hands, they say, do the devil's work
so take just a moment for a simple swain.

To combat the smell of zinc and sulfur
charcoal and disease, get out of the house
for a little while to ward off melancholia, anodyne
to cabin fever and the rancid odor of despair.

Fill in this brief census form, and leave a contact
number so I can reach you on a rainy day.
I would appreciate it awfully, by the way
if you'd come with me today, hand in glove.

THE SYMMETRY OF LOVE

It is bipolar,
from one extreme to another
we live like Venus on the half shell
trying to put our lives together
when love is the marriage of opposites.
It fills us, leaves us dry.

We find it in the oddest places,
a magnitude of a new moon,
the ice in a comet's tail,
the star and the cradle,
this rocking horse of a universe
we ride until we master the bicycle.

Children play at wheelbarrows
among the Chinese lanterns,
spinning cartwheels and lifting
each other up by their soles,
feet don't touch the floor,
dreams bobbing like their heads.

Spilling over their pillows
comes the evening flood,
the dog is twitching nightmares,
the witch waits in the woods,
while in the smile above
the ginger cat is dreaming of
a perfect love.

CALVERTON

No one was in the bunker
at Ramsdale Park that day,
but the dark wind that blew me here
in the shadow of the colliery,
was sinister, as my writing style,
black as a rook's tower.

A woman in a plaid skirt
hobbled on an arthritic cane, entered
the coffee shop, to a scratchy version
of an Eastern European polka song, that
kept playing in the same crooked groove,
as I finished my coffee a man yelled "Eh!"

Pushing my bike ahead of me, I snaked
around the curves, through the green mist,
of the lavender evening ahead casting its scent,
until looking back I saw the lights
of Calverton, falling away, my heart beating
like a canary in the coal mine of my chest.

So I rode away on my bicycle
swerving into the sunset, until I reached
the sign pointing ahead to Calverton,
"Twinned with Longué-Jumelles."
The colliery rose up again, as I pedaled up
George's Hill, derailed like a poet, one foot at a time.

THE LONG ROOM AT
TRINITY COLLEGE, DUBLIN

To walk under the arched ceiling, past row upon row
of gold-bound books, beneath the busts of poets,
clergymen, and scholars presiding like holy ghosts
over the daily rite of this procession speaks volumes.

And then to move among the memories of writers;
Russell, Joyce, and Wilde makes one a child, admiring
Yeats's half-mile trophy, Synge's antique typewriter
and the wood-carved Otway Harp framed in the corner.

To never hear a voice above a whisper, the squeak
of polished leather as people gather at the *Book
of Kells*, this parchment of faces, anxiously turned
into a parliament and chorus of illuminations.

SITTING AT THE SYLVIA BEACH
MEMORIAL READING ROOM AT
SHAKESPEARE AND CO., PARIS

At first, the room is unnaturally quiet,
then a voice says: "You can take a book upstairs
from the library and read until midnight if you like."
It might have been the woman with red hair.
So you climb the stairs dutifully just as others
must have done and the room is thick with dust
and the book jackets are all buttoned up, and so
you pad in like an old retriever over the rug.

Mrs. Dalloway is the title you settle on, nearest
to your head, and then you sit down to read
in the green easy chair, as frayed
at the arm as your sweater. Hours pass
and your eyes wander over the pages as you imagine
the neon light, the houseplant, and the bookshelves
leaning in to listen. Suddenly, a thought is born:
If no one discovers me here I could go blind as Milton.

But no cause for alarm, there are only creaking floors
and a few chairs with lumbago—as long as the siren
you hear making an emergency call comes no closer.
Meanwhile, Mrs. Dalloway lives her life in a respectable
way across the channel. Saint-Michel grows to an uproar,
and the river rats of the Seine begin to move as footsteps
on the stairs, cracks in the ceiling widen to a face.
The curtain is continually stirring as the words beneath
your fingers rise from the page in the needlepoint of lace.

III
LOVE IS A BLUR

Tears are words that need to be written.
—Paulo Coelho

LOVE IS A BLUR

Your hand opens against my back
 and your eyes close, your hair waving to me
  thick as lamb's wool and we seem
   to be dancing while standing still in slow motion.
    Freeze-frame, yet we turn
     on our own pedestal as bride and groom
     on our wedding cake, your ring, with
      its triple garnet crown, turns like
       Orion's Belt pointing toward my Taurus
       as we are held in this ring with
          so much happiness surrounding us.

PAVLOVA'S SLIPPERS

Karpeles Manuscript Museum, Tacoma, Washington

Her pink ballet shoes
with white laces
soles worn down
rest together as one.

After 32 fouettés
the satin pink slippers
of Anna Pavlova
can finally stop.

Off pointe
lay side by side
may her sleeping toes
lie down at last.

A PORTRAIT OF GREAT BRITAIN

She stands in Indian dress
a little girl proud of her heritage
handed down through a grandmother
the railway station her stage
Leeds, Manchester, Piccadilly, London
amid iron Victorian scaffolding
she hangs like a portrait.

Overlap of blue sky, Mehta's eyes
with her eggshell dress
shining through the smoke, soot
of grit like a chit on
British billboards and digital screens
caught out on a cold day
a snapshot of her mother's gaze.

On the Yorkshire Dales, near Leeds
her family nearby as Nina
jumping up and down with her mother
given a chance, her Indian descent
framed against the impersonal
Elizabethan blue imperial sky
where she reigns in saffron.

POETS TABLE ZOOM

Our faces were in boxes that night
Darren's upper right in black
Sue in blue, her hair glowing
Nan with a white background
Cathy with a poster from Italy
mischievous as always
me, with the Brooklyn Bridge
in the background, part in shadow
part in light, all of us polite.

On this last night, missing Ken
we read our poems, one by one
ear cocked, a pen in hand
like a Venetian gallery—
each of us part of the whole
made up a roundtable of poets
together our faces told a story
Dante would put into a canto or
a tapestry weaved by Boccaccio.

POWER OF ONE

If the words aren't enough
blame the poet
who keeps them to himself.

If the world isn't right
blame the politician
but keep voting anyway.

If your weight's not right
blame the scales
that tip the balance of justice.

If your hair's not right
look at yourself in the mirror.
Blame the stylist.

Keep subtracting and soon
you'll find yourself alone,
with no one left to blame.

And that will give you
all the power you need
and blame enough.

MURDER WEAPON

Most of them, I have no doubt,
are kind-hearted law-abiding men who would never
dream of committing murder in private life.
　　　　—George Orwell, "The Lion and
　　　　　　the Unicorn"

It is the silent word
that threatens us,
the polished word
sticking in our throats.

All hint at violence:
the inward-looking glance,
the holes in the ellipsis…
a bulge beneath the overcoat.

All show just enough
to make you sense the instrument,
ill-defined, but poised,
point-blank.

COMPOSTING AND DECONSTRUCTING OF HOPKINS

They both require work
and accumulations of dirt
beneath your nails and thumbs
to grasp a tool by the nib
and shovel too, turning over
a new grave to find there is
life among ruins of the roots
and vines that strangle you.

Verbs that you must cultivate
finding new legs so you can
create a space for life to grow
out of the cracks and broken
concrete poems, something else
may spring, another kind of verse
that will break apart the rhyming
DNA in our bones.

IN THE GLOW OF KINDLE

In the glow of kindle
after the lights are out
and I have extinguished
the candles like Dante's
drop-down screen

to study the hieroglyphs
passed on from the
Rosetta stone, and I am
Diogenes looking for the
one undecipherable man.

Here in the evening
with a lamp by my bed
to find the intelligible
or illegible page that,
rekindled, once again
must be read.

THE DAY KEEPS TRACK

I sit, a blank face
an empty page
in front of me
day ahead on my lap
a peaceful plea of hope

my words are long behind me
soft place of memory
we come to Pearl,
I transfer to my past
look for words
that will fill this book

the spine of thoughts
a man hums through
his teeth like paper
on a comb, a bee's tune
or a poem

blows through me
skin to bone
my eyes like the day
are partly cloudy,
part paradox.

GUITAR

An open-mouthed sounding board
with frets to string and hearts
played upside down, inside out
gives voice like an evening prayer
and all our wishes a cacophony
to be tuned, an opening for air.

I hold against myself, cradle
my body a rocking chair
that touches me as I strum
a melody no one else can hear.
Come sing. Bring your ear—
Listen to the boxwood hum.

HAUSER AND LARA FABIAN'S "CARUSO"

from a concert

His bow raised against her diaphanous
body flowing down radiant chords of her hair
her face in a passionate twist, as she
sings to him with a cello—her "Caruso"
and each and every note becomes—

love song's bursting breath of passionate
longing on a string, as she lifts her head
finds her place, throws back her neck's
white lace to hang against a mirror
where flowers bloom their encores.

THE CHOREOGRAPHIC GIFT

Today my bones knit together
as though lent by some
other frame of being I can't
reconstruct, unbend—bent
double, undone, tortured
like some Hopkins poem—

Or something Yeats dragged in
my room, a sounding board
consul of pain, laid out
on the couch, I think of Cromwell
how he learned to torture men
knew how to apply just pressure.

Then let up, having gained
his confession, guilt by confusion
always difficult, my gift like his
words, a way to orchestrate
in a chorus of pressure points
how I, too, can learn "to sing."

MELCHIOR

I know you burn white sage
for me in your backyard pyre
that your heart often keeps
a log on the fire and that
you have made in your house
an arbor of red leaves overflowing
the headboard of your bed.

You have made of me a believer
the gnostic texts of your
handwriting I keep near my head.
Come, empty your jar
of your holy jinn, I will fill it
with perfume from my tears
make of you my sweet incense.

As to sheltering our dreams
I also know how you
woo me with kind words,
I wish I had sacred beads
to give you but your potion
of frankincense I rub into my skin,
begin our journey once more.

ACKNOWLEDGMENTS

Poems in this collection appear in the following publications:

10 Simple Pleasures
Aria 2020
A Trip to Jerusalem
The Enigmatist
How We Move Toward Light (MoonPath Press, 2018)
Ireland's Eye
Jack Straw Writer's Anthology
Love Is a Blur
Medley
Melange
On Air: KTAH FM
Only Connect Anthology
Open Book Western Washington Poetry Network Anthology
Pennine Ink
*Poetry Chicago World Poetry Day 2025 Mini-Anthology:
     Ars Poetica*
Poets' Table Anthology
Poets West Literary Journal
Raven Chronicles Journal, Vol. 23: Jack Straw Writers
     Program, 1997–2016
Shiny Things (MoonPath Press, 2025)
The Suburban Times
Terra Firma: Sacred Ground, Poems 1970–2022 (MoonPath
     Press, 2022)
Wellberry Prize, First Place

Poems in this collection also appear in the following venues:

MoonPath Press Zoom Reading Series
Poet's House Showcase, NYC

ABOUT THE ARTIST

Sadie Murazzo is a Jersey girl, vis-à-vis California, but has Northwest breeding to go with it. This is her first book cover.

In Sadie's own words, "My earliest recollection of art was the art I did in kindergarten of children playing ring-around-the-rosy. Back then and for several years, my art was realistic until I gravitated to symbolic line drawings, which in this book is an example of a computer manipulated line drawing. At present, my work has taken the form of abstract, black-and-white cut-paper collage, but no matter the style, art is my life!"

ABOUT THE AUTHOR

Crowed is Michael Magee's fifth collection of poetry and a Sally Albiso Prize finalist. In this collection he goes back to his Celtic roots, family, and friends and pays homage to those he's learned from.

His most recent third third and fourth collections were *Shiny Things* and *Budapest After Dark*, published in 2025. His plays and poetry have been produced here and in England and Greece.

New work appears in *Open Book: Western Washington Poets Network Anthology* and *Cirque*. He conducts writing workshops and appears on KTAH FM RadioTacoma, VerseDaily.Org, and *The Writer's Almanac*.

Michael's poems reflect his interest in nature, theatre, music, literature, and travel. His mentors and friends have been David Wagoner, Ben Drake, and William Matchett, professors emeriti at the University of Washington. His musical influences include: Franz Liszt, Chopin, Lou Reed, Leonard Cohen, Marianne Faithfull, and Townes Van Zandt.

He has lived in England and traveled in Ireland as well as Hungary, Morocco, and Turkey. He is recipient of a Jack Straw Residency and lives in Tacoma, Washington.

Also by Michael Magee

Shiny Things (MoonPath Press, 2025)

Terra Firma (MoonPath Press, 2022)

How We Move Toward Light (MoonPath Press, 2018)

Cinders of My Better Angels (MoonPath Press, 2011)

www.ingramcontent.com/pod-product-compliance
Lightning Source LLC
Chambersburg PA
CBHW020756130626
46554CB00006B/2211